IMAGES OF LONDON

BRENTFORD AND CHISWICK PUBS

LITERARY SPIRIT SERIES No 8.

BURLINGTON ARMS, CHISWICK:—
Dating from the 15th Century, it still retains the charac-
teristics of a typical riverside inn of the period when
Chiswick was the country haunt of many of the intellectual
celebrities of the past two centuries.

Johnnie Walker: "A Hogarth drawing proclaims the Age."

Shade of Hogarth: "Yes, and every bottle of your product carries it always."

JOHN WALKER & SONS, LTD., SCOTCH WHISKY DISTILLERS, KILMARNOCK, SCOTLAND

IMAGES OF LONDON

BRENTFORD AND CHISWICK PUBS

GILLIAN CLEGG

TEMPUS

To all those with whom I have spent many happy hours in the pubs of Brentford and Chiswick.

Frontispiece: The Burlington Arms, Church Street, Chiswick, shown in an advertisement for John Walker & Sons which appeared in *Punch*, 1924.

First published 2005

Tempus Publishing Limited
The Mill, Brimscombe Port,
Stroud, Gloucestershire, GL5 2QG
www.tempus-publishing.com

British Library Cataloguing in Publication Data.
A catalogue record for this book is available from the British Library.

ISBN 0 7524 3723 2

Typesetting and origination by Tempus Publishing Limited.
Printed in Great Britain.

Contents

Acknowledgements

I am particularly grateful to Carolyn Hammond for her help with the research, to Peter Hammond who scanned most of the illustrations and to David Marles for taking photographs. Thanks also go to Peter Downes and Brian Prior who lent postcards from their collections and to the following for their different, but invaluable, assistance: Celia Cotton, Fuller, Smith & Turner (Tony Johnson and Georgina Wald), Sam Gleadon, Catherine McCallum, Janet McNamara, James Marshall, Victoria Northwood, Jonathan Oates, Brian Pipe, Shirley Seaton, Catherine Taylor. Also to my husband, Patrick McHugh, for his patience and support.

Most of the illustrations in the book come from the Chiswick Local Studies collection and I am grateful to the London Borough of Hounslow for permission to reproduce them. Other illustrations (identified by the page number and 'a' for the upper picture or 'b' for the lower picture) are printed by permission of: the *Brentford, Chiswick & Isleworth Times* (35a, 40b, 39a, 42b, 50b, 55a, 63, 66a, 78a, 85b, 87a, 91b, 100a, 104b, 109a, 112a, 113b, 122, 123b); Ralph Clifton (72a); Peter Downes (25, 27, 32b, 55b, 56a, 57, 59a, 65, 70b, 76a, 83b, 101, 111a, 123a, 124a); Heather Duberley (96b); Fuller, Smith & Turner (12, 14a, 14b, 35b, 36b, 47a, 60, 73a, 82b, 88b, 120a); J.C. Gillham (44b, 86a); Paul Gorringe (77a); Eleanor Greeves (15, 126); Gunnersbury Park Museum (13b, 39b); London Borough of Ealing (108a, 108b); Frank and Gerardine McBrearty (46b); Janet McNamara (82a, 86b, 89b, 95a, 96a, 98b); David Marles (10, 28b, 29a, 29b, 37a, 37b, 48a, 48b, 67a, 67b, 72b, 75a, 75b, 81b, 92a, 93b, 100b, 102b, 103a, 105b, 112b, 115b, 116b, 120b, 121a, 121b, 125a, 125b, 127b); Catherine Masterman (107a); His Grace the Duke of Northumberland (26a); Jayson Perfect (36a); Brian Prior (16a, 34b, 40a, 41, 49, 53, 103b, 106b, 109b, 110, 113a, 117, 118a); David Scuffam (9); Mrs Smyth (79, 80a, 80b, 81a); James Wisdom (43b, 105a).

In some cases it has not been possible to identify or contact the copyright holder, so apologies if any copyrights have been infringed.

Note: The dates given in this book for when pubs were first licensed or opened can only be approximate. The licensing records for Brentford and Chiswick only list pub names from 1722 and complete sets of licensing lists no longer survive. The earliest trade directories for this area don't appear before the early nineteenth century and they were only published in certain years. Some pubs will be earlier than indicated but have changed their name, which is not always easy to identify from the records, and beerhouses were not licensed initially, or given names.

Introduction

In 1888 there were sixty-four pubs in Brentford, thirty-nine of which were along the main road between Kew Bridge and Brentford End, a distance of just over one and a half miles. Today Brentford has only twenty-three pubs (nine along the main road). Chiswick has fared better with twenty-one pubs now compared to thirty-nine in 1888.

The 1880s and 1890s were the golden age of the public house and pub numbers have been steadily declining ever since – all part of a move towards fewer but better pubs. Interestingly, though, statistics show that the more pubs there are, the less drunkenness there is!

'Public House' is a term only conjured up in the nineteenth century to embrace the various types of drinking establishment – alehouses, taverns, inns, gin palaces, beer shops, and so on. These terms are now used interchangeably but earlier these were very different types of establishment: alehouses sold only ale (and later beer); taverns sold wine; ginshops, spirits; beerhouses, beer and cider, whereas inns provided accommodation as well as food and drink. It's easier to understand the expression 'public house' when you realise that many early boozers were just ordinary domestic dwellings.

Pubs were much more than places to drink, though. They were venues where people could watch or take part in activities such as wrestling, bear and bull baiting, boxing, bowling, skittles, cock fighting, juggling, miracle and mystery plays, and later attend concerts, balls, music halls and lectures. Business transactions were conducted in pubs and political and other meetings held. Many also doubled as coroner's courts, auction houses and even mortuaries.

Brief history

The Romans introduced the first embryonic pubs to England, their *tabernae* (from which the word tavern comes) served wine and were denoted by a bush of vine leaves displayed above the door (the first inn signs). Alehouses, which have been around since at least Saxon times, were often just private homes where people came to buy ale, which was often brewed by the householders themselves. Permanent alehouses start to appear in significant numbers in the thirteenth century and in 1393 King Richard II decreed that all alehouses must display an 'alestake' (*see* page 9). Alestakes extended into the road and could be a traffic hazard, so by the seventeenth century a drinking establishment was denoted by lattice-work, before painted pub signs became commonplace.

Ale is made from barley, beer is ale to which hops have been added. Hops were introduced in medieval times and act as a preservative which means the brew keeps longer. Beer became the more common drink in the early seventeenth century. Water being none too safe to drink, ale or beer was the staple drink for everyone, including children. Many people drank 'small beer', a weaker brew made from a second boiling of the barley mash.

Taverns, which served wine and food, were more upmarket than alehouses and mainly found in towns. They were particularly popular from the sixteenth to late eighteenth century but their demise came when wine could be obtained from other outlets.

Inns grew up in medieval times to feed and shelter the growing number of people making pilgrimages (previously, most pilgrims had stayed in monasteries). The heyday of the inn was during the coaching era of the eighteenth and early nineteenth centuries. Three thousand coaches pounded the roads of England in 1836. Travellers going west were no doubt grateful to find succour in inns like the Pack Horse in Chiswick or the Three Pigeons in Brentford before attempting the hazardous ride across Hounslow Heath, a notorious haunt of highwaymen.

The consumption of gin (introduced from the Netherlands in 1586) began to grow dramatically and in the 1820s gave rise to a new breed of drinking den – the 'dram shop', 'gin shop' or 'gin palace'. These differed from alehouses, taverns and inns in that they offered no seats, no food and no service. People drank standing up, served from a 'bar counter'. This was an innovation which became a universal feature of later pubs. To attract customers, the decor was deliberately designed to be eye-catching – lots of plate glass, polished brass and carved mahogany. This too was to influence the design of later Victorian pubs.

Perhaps with the intention of discouraging gin drinking, the Beer Act was passed in 1830. This abolished all duty on beer and allowed any householder to sell beer and cider from the premises on payment of a two-guinea licence fee to the Excise. Beer shops mushroomed, particularly in areas like Brentford with its large working population. However, the Act was not a success since it took control of liquor licensing out of the hands of the local magistrates who monitored drinking establishments and had the power to withdraw or refuse licences to those they felt didn't come up to scratch. Beer shops were brought back under the control of the magistrates in 1869.

The number of pubs grew and grew during the nineteenth century and by the 1890s they had become bigger, brighter, gayer and more glitzy than they had ever been before, or are ever likely to be again. When Victorian pubs are mentioned it is probably the decorated glass that springs to mind and several pubs in Brentford and Chiswick still retain their attractive glass.

Then came the crash – pubs had grown too big too fast and alcohol consumption was not increasing. Landlords had over-extended themselves on rebuilding and refurbishing and were unable to pay off loans borrowed from the breweries. At the beginning of the twentieth century many landlords went bust. This benefited the breweries which had been steadily acquiring pubs. By 1915 the brewers owned 95 per cent of all pubs.

Developments in the twentieth century include the introduction of 'keg' beer (pasteurised sterilised beer) in the 1940s. This keeps longer, is easier to handle and travels better. However, many people dislike its flavour and fizziness. Traditional beer in 'casks' came to be known as 'real ale' and to promote it CAMRA (the Campaign for Real Ale) was founded in 1971. Lager, which had been around since the 1900s, had become a favourite tipple by the 1960s. In the later twentieth century the breweries themselves

An alestake drawn from a fourteenth-century manuscript. This not only showed where ale could be purchased but alerted the ale-conner, a parish official whose duty it was to ensure the quality of the brew was good enough to sell.

began massive mergers, although luckily some smaller breweries survived intact and we are proud to have one of the best in Chiswick – Fuller, Smith & Turner's award-winning Griffin Brewery. By 1989 six big breweries provided 77 per cent of the nation's beer and owned 34,000 pubs between them. In an attempt to make the beer market more competitive the government decreed that the big brewers must divest themselves of any pubs they owned in excess of 2,000. This has caused many pubs to close and others to be bought up by property developers or other companies in the leisure market. Many former pubs have been turned into restaurants or 'gastro-pubs'. However, the pub has now largely lost its stigma as a place of drunkenness and become more acceptable with its family-friendly policy and improved standard of food. But we must patronise our pubs if we want them to remain.

Pub names

Before most people could read there was little point displaying a written name above a shop or pub, so painted signs were used instead. Until the seventeenth century pub names were very simple – Lion, Bull, Swan, etc., but, later, words were combined

Inn sign of the Waterman's Arms, Ferry Lane Brentford. This shows the coat of arms of the Company of Watermen and Lightermen.

together, perhaps to distinguish one pub from another or because two pubs had been joined. Unlike Ireland, where pub names are usually those of a past or present landlord, English pub names derive from a multitude of sources. The following lists some of these, with examples from pubs in Brentford and Chiswick.

Animal names are very common, e.g. the Packhorse and Talbot (the talbot was a hunting dog), as are names of kings and queens, particularly George IV. Famous people feature, e.g. Lord Nelson, as do names from occupations, e.g. the Waggon and Horses and geographical names like the Globe. The English love of bell ringing is reflected in the Six Bells, and fondness for beer in the Barley Mow (a 'mow' is a heap of barley). Some names have religious connotations – two former Brentford pubs the Angel and the Salutation derive from the Annunciation.

Very many pub signs are heraldic in origin. The name the Red Lion, for instance, (there have been four in our area) is not derived from the animal but from the 'Lion *gules*' (the heraldic term for a red lion). Emblems of royalty give rise to the names of pubs such as the Crown and the King's Arms. Coats of arms feature in many other pub names, such as the Mawson Arms, the Waterman's Arms and the Bricklayers' Arms. One Chiswick pub has a unique name – The City Barge, so called in honour of the City of London Navigation Committee's ceremonial barge which was then moored by the pub.

Pubs have often had their names changed but this became a fad in the later twentieth century, some pubs being given fatuous new names such as the Rat and Parrot for Chiswick's once great coaching inn, the Roebuck (now the Bird Cage), and the Orange Kipper for the perfectly respectably named Railway Tavern in Bollo Lane (now the Bollo).

Gillian Clegg
August 2005

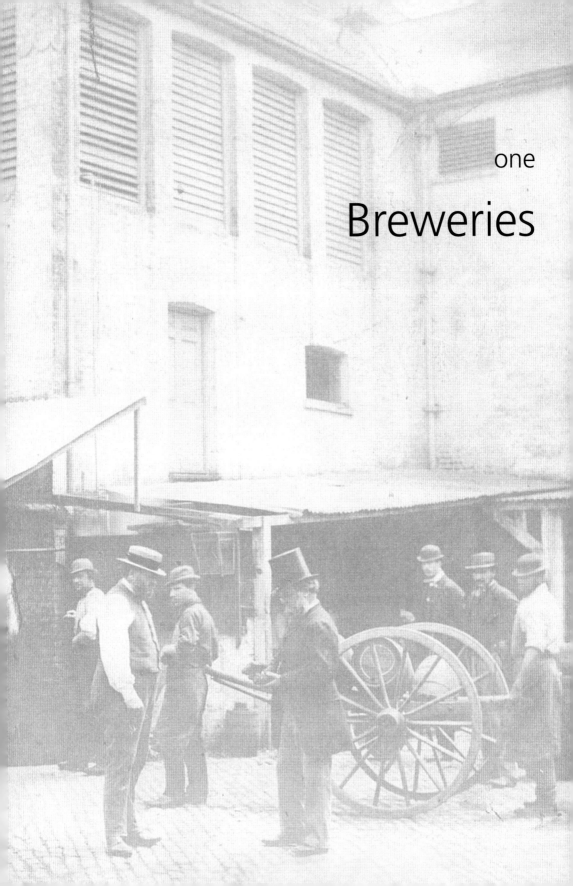

one

Breweries

The entrance to Fuller, Smith & Turner's Griffin Brewery which stands between the A4 and Chiswick Mall. Brewing has been taking place on this site since at least 1701 when the brewery was bought by Thomas Mawson. He sold it to a Chiswick family called Thompson in 1782. John Fuller joined the firm in 1829, providing a much needed injection of capital. In 1845 his son, John Bird Fuller, acquired the brewery and, along with Henry Smith, of Romford brewers Ind Smith, Smith's son Henry and son-in-law John Turner, formed Fuller, Smith & Turner. Descendants of these families still run the brewery today. It became a private limited company in 1929 and went public in 1981/2. The brewery was named the Griffin in 1816, when the Thompson family unofficially adopted the Griffin name from a brewery in the City belonging to Meux and Reid when this partnership broke up. Legal wrangles, though, prevented Fuller, Smith & Turner using the name as its trademark until 1892. This picture shows the wisteria which clads the brewery wall. This is the oldest wisteria plant in England. When the first wisteria was brought to Kew Gardens from China in 1816, a cutting was given to the brewery since it supplied beer to Kew. The Kew plant perished while the brewery plant flourished.

Right: An advertisement for Fuller, Smith & Turner's Griffin Brewery, *c.* 1895. The company now owns over 240 pubs and its beers have won CAMRA'S Beer of the Year award five times over the last fourteen years.

Below: Tommy Wood, Fuller, Smith & Turner's last cooper going through the coopers' initiation ceremony known as 'trussing in' on completing his apprenticeship in the early 1960s. When Fuller's replaced wooden barrels with aluminium casks, Tommy Wood joined brewer Young and Co.

Telegrams: FULLER, CHISWICK.
Telephone: 838, HAMMERSMITH
(2 Lines)

FULLER AND Co

GRIFFIN BREWERY

CHISWICK
MIDDLESEX.

DIRECTIONS FOR THE MANAGEMENT OF BEERS AND EMPTY CASKS.

WHEN placing the cask for tapping, care should be taken that the front is slightly lower than the back; and when it requires tilting, gently raise the back and block up firmly.

The temperature of the cellar should be about 50°.

When empty, the cask should be corked and pegged directly, and returned immediately.

Employees of Fuller, Smith & Turner, with the tools of their trade, outside the Griffin Brewery in the early twentieth century.

A Fuller's dray, *c.* 1900. Horses were largely replaced by steam vehicles early in the twentieth century and these in turn were replaced by motor vehicles after the Second World War.

Opposite: The Lamb Brewery building in 1952. This picture by Tom Greeves, looking down Chiswick's Church Street, is drawn from where the Hogarth Roundabout is today. The brewery building (put up in 1901) is the tower in the centre of the picture, the building on the right-hand side is the Victorian Feathers pub. The Sich family were running the Lamb Brewery by at least 1790. It was practically next door to the Griffin Brewery belonging to its rivals, Fuller, Smith & Turner. Sich & Co. sold out to the Isleworth Brewery in 1920. Two years later the Isleworth Brewery was bought by Watney, Coombe and Reid, later Watney, Mann Truman. This became part of Grand Metropolitan which now belongs to Diageo. The Lamb Brewery building was used by the Standard Yeast Co. until 1952, after which it was converted to offices.

Above: On the right are stores belonging to the Lamb Brewery in Church Street in the 1920s. They extended under the house now known as the Guardship. Beer was pumped through pipes to the stores' cellars. Here it was kept in barrels for up to a month before being delivered. Bottled beer would also have been stored here, and probably hops and other materials as well.

Below: Whitbread's bottling stores in 1926. They were in Essex Place where Sainsbury's is today. They were built in 1914 but promptly taken over by the government for the storage of furniture, etc. from hotels in the West End which had been requisitioned as wartime government offices. The stores were handed back to Whitbread's in 1921 and bottling continued on the site until 1983.

Wm. Gomm & Son,

PALE ALE & PORTER BREWERS,

Bee Hive Brewery, Brentford.

Right: Advertisement for the Beehive Brewery in 1899. Wm Gomm & Son were selling beer from at least 1838, probably their own brew. Gomm's original premises were behind where the Beehive pub is now in Brentford High Street. In 1877 Gomm's purchased the Grand Junction Brewery in Catherine Wheel Yard (now Road) and on this site built the new and expanded Beehive Brewery.

Below: Delivery cart belonging to Wm Gomm & Son of Brentford's Beehive Brewery in 1907.

All our Beers are Brewed from the finest selected Malt and Choicest Hops.

PRICE LIST FOR PRIVATE FAMILIES.

		Kils. 18 Gals.	Firkin 9 Gals.	Pin 4½ Gals.
X	MILD ALE	14s. 0d.	7s. 0d.	3s. 9d.
A.K.	LIGHT DINNER ALE	18s. 0d.	9s. 0d.	4s. 6d.
XXI	INTERMEDIATE	20s. 0d.	10s. 0d.	5s. 0d.
P.B.A.	PALE ALE	24s. 0d.	12s. 0d.	6s. 0d.
A.P.	RICH BITTER ALE	27s. 0d.	13s. 6d.	6s. 9d.
XXXXS	STOCK ALE	30s. 0d.	15s. 0d.	7s. 6d.
P	PORTER	18s. 0d.	9s. 0d.	4s. 6d.
S.P.	COOPER	20s. 0d.	10s. 0d.	5s. 0d.
S.	STOUT	24s. 0d.	12s. 0d.	6s. 0d.
D.S.	DOUBLE STOUT (for Invalids and Nursing)	27s. 0d.	13s. 6d.	6s. 9d.

BOTTLED BEERS.

	Per doz. Pts.	Per doz. ½ Pts.
LIGHT DINNER ALE	2s. 6d.	1s. 6d.
PALE BITTER ALE	3s. 6d.	2s. 0d.
COOPER	2s. 6d.	1s. 6d.
INVALID STOUT	3s. 6d.	2s. 0d.

N.B.—A Discount of 3d. per 4½, 6d. per 9, 1s. per 18 gallons, and 3d. per Dozen Pint Bottles will be allowed for cash paid strictly on Delivery.

THE BEEHIVE BREWERY.
BRENTFORD, W.

This Plan is published for reference only and although believed to be correct, its accuracy is in no way guaranteed.

— Scale 30 Feet = 1 Inch.—

Plan of the Beehive Brewery, Brentford, drawn for its sale by auction in 1908. Fuller, Smith & Turner bought the brewery and its thirty-four pubs.

Opposite above: Early twentieth-century beer labels for Wm Gomm & Son's Beehive Brewery.

Opposite below: Advertisement for Ind Coope & Co. in 1899. This Romford brewer had established a delivery depot at Northumberland Wharf in Brentford by 1873.

18

Ind, Coope & Co.'s

ROMFORD

ALES, STOUTS,

AND

PORTER

IN

$4\frac{1}{2}$, 9, and 18 Gallon Casks.

Price . Lists . on . Application . to

LOCAL OFFICE,

184, HIGH STREET,

BRENTFORD.

The Royal Brewery, Brentford High Street, in the early 1900s. This stood where Watermans Park is today. Brewing was taking place on this site by at least 1735 when it was known as the British Brewery. The name was changed to the Red Lion Brewery in 1825 and it was re-christened the Royal Brewery by no less a person than a King of England! By 1829 the brewery was owned by Messrs Booth & Co., distillers, of Clerkenwell. Booth's chairman was Felix Booth (later knighted) who, in that year, contributed £17,000 to the expedition undertaken by explorer Capt James Ross to discover the North West Passage from the Atlantic to the Pacific oceans. In gratitude for Booth's generosity, King William IV visited the brewery and expressed a wish that it should change its name and also conferred the right to use and display the Royal Coat of Arms. King William apparently named the brewery himself by breaking a bottle of wine on the wall of the counting house.

Opposite above: Advertisement for Royal Light Bitter Ale, described in an account of the firm around 1905 as a 'recently introduced speciality ... a non deposit bottle'.

Opposite below: Advertisement for the Royal Brewery in 1877. The brewery had been acquired by Carrington & Whitehurst in 1852 and sold to Gibbon & Croxford in 1861. In 1880 it was bought by Montague Ballard who sold it in 1922 to Style & Winch, together with 102 pubs and off-licences. Brewing ceased on the site in 1923 and the buildings were demolished in 1926 to make way for an extension to the Brentford gasworks.

ROYAL
Light Bitter
ALE ..

2/6 Per Dozen

IN BOTTLE
(DELIVERED).

Royal Brewery,

OLD BRENTFORD.

GIBBON & CROXFORD,

ALE AND PORTER BREWERS.

Prices to Private Families, net for Cash.

	9 Gallons. s. d.	18 Gallons. s. d.
Light Bitter Ales, AK...	9 0	18 0
No. 1 Mild Ale	7 6	15 0
No. 2 Mild Ale	10 0	20 0
No. 3 Mild Ale	15 0	30 0
Porter	9 0	18 0
Stout	12 0	24 0
Pale Ale	12 6	25 0

**DRAYS DELIVER DAILY IN THE WHOLE DISTRICT
EMBRACED BY THIS DIRECTORY.**

The AK and Nursing Stout in 6-gallon Casks if required.

ALL ORDERS WILL MEET WITH PROMPT ATTENTION.

THOMAS TEARLE,
STAR BREWERY,
BRENTFORD.

Bottled Ales and Stout of all kinds.

Price per Cask of Nine Gallons.

	£	s	d
XXXX Ale	£0	15	0
XXX ditto	0	12	0
XX ditto	0	9	0
Pale Ale	0	10	0
Table Ale	0	7	0
Table Beer	0	5	0

Bottled Ale and Stout per Dozen.

	QUARTS.		PINTS.
Burton or Scotch Ale	9s.	....	5s.
Irish Stout	7s.	....	4s.
Pale Ale	7s.	....	4s.

Above: The yard of the Royal Brewery in the early 1900s. The brewery's premises extended from the High Street to the river where there was a landing wharf for loading and unloading goods and materials which were conveyed by water.

Left: Advertisement for the Star Brewery, Brentford, in 1848. The brewery was in Boston Manor Road. It is not listed in the trade directories after 1852 but as several other breweries in Boston Manor Road are listed perhaps it changed its name. Thomas Tearle also had a brewery in Kingston.

two

Coaching Inns

The Red Lion, No. 197 Brentford High Street, in the early 1900s. The pub on the left in this photograph of a busy Brentford High Street looks quite ordinary but in Brentford's heyday it was on the corner of Market Place and was one of the major pubs in the town. It was in 'the Lion', in 1446, that Henry VI held a Chapter of the Garter at which two new Knights of the Garter were appointed. The Great Room of the Red Lion was where the magistrates sat and dispensed justice in the seventeenth century. In 1670 the magistrates changed their venue to the Three Pigeons but returned two years later after this wheedling note from the landlord William Parish:

> Gentlemen I am heartily sorry that your worships have taken distaste and left your old inn. I am sensible that it was not without cause. If your worships please to return again I shall take it for a very great favour...

The Manorial Court also met in the Red Lion, but again there was a problem. In 1755 the Manorial Court Roll says 'Court never to be held again at the Lion while Hancock keeps it because he is an imposing fellow and gave us a very bad dinner'. In 1762 divine service was held in the Red Lion while St Lawrence's church was being rebuilt. The pub closed around 1928.

Opposite above: The Angel Inn, London Road, by James Pollard (1797-1859). The inn is first mentioned in 1557 when two prisoners being brought to London were put up at the inn for the night. On the right-hand side of the picture is the Brentford tollgate, in use when the main road to the west of England was a turnpike road during the eighteenth and early nineteenth centuries.

Opposite below: The Angel in 1972. The old pub was rebuilt in 1935 and its name changed to the Park Tavern in 1989. It closed in 2001; the building was demolished in 2002 and replaced by the flats called Syon Court.

25

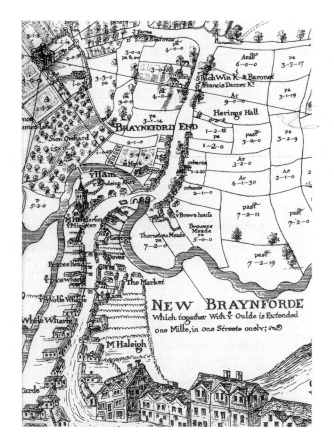

Drawn & Etched by H.W. Wilkins, June 1849.

OLD STABLING OF THE "THREE PIGEONS", BRENTFORD.

THIS INN FREQUENTED BY SHAKESPEARE & BEN JONSON.

Pl. 38 Vol. III

The Three Pigeons, Market Place, *c.* 1905. Brentford market can be seen to the right (Brentford had a thriving market from 1306-1933). The Three Pigeons was Brentford's premier pub, reputedly visited by William Shakespeare and Ben Johnson. It was originally known as the Crown (recorded as such in 1436) and sometimes also known as the Three Doves. Early in the seventeenth century it was kept by John Lowin, an actor and a friend of Shakespeare; who must have known Brentford since he mentions the town in *The Merry Wives of Windsor*. His contemporary, Ben Johnson refers to the pub in his play *The Alchemist* (1610): 'We will turn our courage to Braynford – westward, My bird of the night to the Pigeons'. In the eighteenth and early nineteenth centuries the Middlesex Magistrates Court was held in the pub, as were sessions of the manorial court. In 1840, when Queen Victoria and Prince Albert passed through Brentford on their wedding day, the Three Pigeons prepared a feast for the local schoolchildren and the pub was illuminated in the evening. Local historian Thomas Faulkner described the pub in 1845 (before it was rebuilt) thus: 'still in its ancient state, having about twenty sitting and sleeping apartments, connected by a projecting gallery at the back, and communicating by several staircases to the attics with numerous dark closets and passages'. The pub's licence was not renewed after 1915 but the building remained until 1950. Now (2005) a tile shop stands on its site.

Opposite above: The Lion in Market Place shown on Moses Glover's map of 1635, along with other Brentford pubs. In the sixteenth century, the pub had a lively landlady called Jyl of Brentford who is recorded in a ballad thus: 'There dwelt a widow of homely sort/Honest in substance and full of sport...' Petty Sessions records show that one Richard White threatened to 'fire' the Red Lion Inn in 1668.

Opposite below: The stabling behind the Three Pigeons in 1848. The stables stretched right back to the river Brent and had room for seventy horses, a coach house and an ostler's dwelling place. The building on the left is Brentford's old market house. This was taken down in 1850 when the Town Hall (now the Magistrates Court) was built.

Above: The Coach and Horses, London Road, in the early nineteenth century. Dating back to the seventeenth century, this is the only original coaching inn to remain in Brentford and Chiswick. It is mentioned in Charles Dickens's *Oliver Twist* as the place where the cart put down Bill Sykes and Oliver on their way to commit the burglary in Chertsey.

Left: Doorway of the Coach and Horses in 2005. The inn was bought by Young & Co. from the Percy family (Dukes of Northumberland) in the early nineteenth century. It is now the only Young's pub in Brentford and Chiswick.

Right: Stained glass in the window of the Coach and Horses, portraying its name, but why is there only one horse?!

Below: The Coach and Horses, 2005. The bay window allowed travellers waiting for coaches to watch for their approach from either direction.

The *Quicksilver* Royal Mail coach passing the Star and Garter by James Pollard, 1835. This old inn near Kew Bridge was licensed by at least 1759 and in 1768 was the venue for the supporters of one of the candidates in the Middlesex Elections (polling was held in Brentford). Details of the election expenses still survive and show that the Star and Garter billed the candidate £247 for entertainment plus compensation for damages caused in the ensuing riots of this rowdy election. This amount was more than double the bill charged by any other Brentford pub. The Star and Garter was owned by Fuller, Smith & Turner from 1882, but ceased to be a pub in 1983 when it was converted into offices, although the original facade was retained.

Opposite above: The rear of the Castle Hotel, Nos 207-208 Brentford High Street in the early nineteenth century. Known as the Harrow in 1614, it was one of Brentford's major inns. It was badly damaged in 1768 by supporters of one of the candidates during the riotous Middlesex Elections held in Brentford, and, in 1823, was almost completely destroyed by a dreadful fire. It was rebuilt with extensive stabling at the rear.

Opposite below: An advertisement for the Castle Hotel after rebuilding (with a theatre incorporated) in 1907. The proprietor, Mr Fred W. Bird, an ex-actor, was a versatile man who combined his landlordly duties with the roles of stage manager, leading man, scene painter, box-office manager and usher! The Castle was closed in 1936 and the building later demolished. A modern block containing flats and shops is on its site.

Star & Garter Hotel

..AND..

Prince's Theatre, Kew Bridge.

CAPTAIN W. T. PURKISS, V.D., PROPRIETOR.

Masonic and other Banquets on the shortest notice.	Wines, Spirits, Malt Liquors, and Cigars OF THE FINEST QUALITY.	Dinners, · · Luncheons, · · Teas, · &c., &c. ·

LARGE ROOMS FOR

MEETINGS, CONCERTS, BALLS

AND

THEATRICAL ENTERTAINMENTS.

Stabling, Pretty Garden,

Bowls, Skittles, Billiards.

ORDERS BY POST ATTENDED TO.

The Bohemia Head, Chiswick High Road in the eighteenth century. The man bowing to his customers is almost certainly Mr John Gibson, who was the landlord from 1763 to 1766. Sometimes known as the 'King of Bohemia' or the 'Sign of the Bohemia', this old pub, which is recorded in 1632, was probably named after the Elector Palatine and King of Bohemia who married the daughter of James I in 1613. The pub's large cellars are said to have been the hiding place of some of the conspirators who plotted to assassinate King William III in Chiswick in 1696 (the plot failed). It ceased to be a pub towards the end of the eighteenth century and was converted into three houses in one of which Italian writer and patriot Ugo Foscolo ended his days. The building was demolished in 1901.

Opposite above: Advertisement for the Star and Garter, Kew Bridge, in 1899. The Prince's Theatre was in the garden of the pub. It was called the Prince's Hall and had been a swimming pool, roller-skating rink, dance hall, cinema and finally a film studio before becoming the Q Theatre between 1924 and 1956.

Opposite below: The Star and Garter in 1904. Kew Bridge was a tram terminus. Behind the tram in the centre can be seen the pinnacle atop the large fountain which stood on this spot where an open-air market was held between 1888 and 1893. The fountain was removed to the Western International Market premises in Southall in 1974. Local residents are petitioning for its return.

'The Roebuck Inn, Turnham Green' by James Pollard, 1825. The private 'drag' of Mr J.F. Sharp is shown standing outside the pub which is now known as the Bird Cage. The Roebuck was licensed from at least 1732 and was where the Manorial Court usually held their meetings in the eighteenth century.

The Roebuck in 1890. The pub was known for its fine bowling green and its extensive stabling, part of which can be glimpsed through the archway. This building was demolished in 1890 and replaced by the present building. In 2005 the pub belonged to the Spirit Group.

One of the roebucks on the pediments of the Bird Cage (formerly Roebuck) pub, photographed in 1971. The animal testifies to the pub's true name which has been changed many times. It was re-christened the Chiswick Eyot in 1983, reverted back to the Roebuck in 1989 but was renamed the Rat and Parrot in 1996 (despite protests from local residents) becoming the Bird Cage in 2002.

The George IV, No. 185 Chiswick High Road, when Joseph Van was the landlord between 1887 and 1913. It was licensed by at least 1777 as Lord Boston's Arms, but called the Boston Arms from 1790 until sometime after 1820, when George IV ascended the throne. Fuller, Smith & Turner had acquired the pub by 1826 and in 1838 George Cloud was running an omnibus service to the City from the George.

Above: The George IV won Fuller, Smith & Turner's Local Pub of the Year award in 2004. Here, manager Jayson Perfect displays the award. Jayson was appointed manager in 1999 at the age of nineteen – Fuller, Smith & Turner's youngest ever manager.

Left: The interior of the George IV in the 1990s.

Above: The George IV in 2005. The pub was rebuilt 1931/2.

Right: Inn sign of the George IV in 2005. A storeroom converted into a function suite in 2002 is now headliners comedy club [*sic*] with live comedy shows at weekends, salsa dancing, live music and other events during the week.

The Old Pack Horse, No. 434 Chiswick High Road, in the nineteenth century. This pub, on the corner of Acton Lane, was licensed by at least 1759 as the West Country Pack Horse. The name was changed to the Lower Pack Horse in 1790 and to simply the Pack Horse by 1811. Local historians, including this one, have confused this pub with the pub now called the Packhorse and Talbot (*see* page 41) which was known as the Pack Horse until 1811. However, new research reveals that many events ascribed to one pub actually happened at the other!

Opposite above: The Old Pack Horse in 1880. It has been a Fuller, Smith & Turner pub since 1808.

Opposite below: Part of the interior of the Old Pack Horse photographed in 1990.

The Packhorse and Talbot, No. 145 (previously No. 173) Chiswick High Road, *c.* 1908. The name of the landlord J.H. Squires is displayed more prominently than either the name of the pub or the brewery! Squires bought a sixty-year lease on the pub in 1896. This is a venerable old Chiswick pub which was called simply the Pack Horse until 1811 and which has frequently been confused with the Old Pack Horse (*see* page 38). A trader's token (these were used instead of coins) dating to 1699 has been found inscribed with the words 'John Holland at Ye Pack Hors in Turnham Green'. In 1696 some of the people who were plotting to assassinate King William III in Wellesley Road met in this pub. In 1725, when the highwayman Jonathan Wild was on trial, he called as a witness Hays of the Pack Horse, Turnham Green. The pub was also the meeting place of the Brentford Turnpike Trust between 1764 and 1776. In 1800, when King George III was travelling across Turnham Green on his journey from London to Windsor, his carriage nearly overturned and a postilion was injured. The postilion was taken to the Pack Horse and put to bed.

Opposite above: The Old Pack Horse in the early 1900s, before it was rebuilt in 1910 to a design by local architect Thomas Henry Nowell Parr. Parr was the architect and surveyor of Brentford Urban District Council who also had a private practice, mainly designing public houses.

Opposite below: A griffin in the stonework on the side of the Old Pack Horse.

Left: A customer's bill of 1799 from the Pack Horse (later the Packhorse and Talbot). It was a popular stopping-off place for travellers along the main road, including Horace Walpole who used to feed his horses here when travelling from Twickenham to London.

Below: Interior of the Packhorse and Talbot in 1970. The original pub had been rebuilt in the 1920s. It now belongs to the Spirit Group which purchased the retail division of Scottish & Newcastle in 2003.

The Packhorse & Talbot,

HIGH ROAD, CHISWICK.

J. H. SQUIRES, JUN., Proprietor.

Noted House for Luncheons from 1 to 3 o'clock.

[[ESTABLISHED OVER 100½ YEARS.

Advertisement for the Packhorse and Talbot, showing the interior, *c.* 1905. In 1782 landlord Joseph Richardson published an advertisement to 'respectfully acquaint his friends and the public in general that he has built a very spacious and elegant room for assemblies and the entertaining of the gentlest and largest companies'.

Inn sign of the Packhorse and Talbot in 1983. Pack horses were used to transport goods from place to place. Talbots were hunting dogs, probably used to protect the merchandise.

H. ROPER, Wine and Spirit Merchant,

"The Crown Inn," GUNNERSBURY.

Noted Old Posting House.

Mr. H. ROPER.

Advertisement for the Crown Inn, No. 475 Chiswick High Road, *c.* 1905. It was a large pub, licensed by at least 1759 and belonged to the Royal Brewery (*see* Chapter 1).

The Crown Inn was rebuilt in the 1920s with assembly rooms. This photograph by J.C. Gillham was taken in 1957, just before the pub was demolished to make way for an enlargement of Chiswick Roundabout.

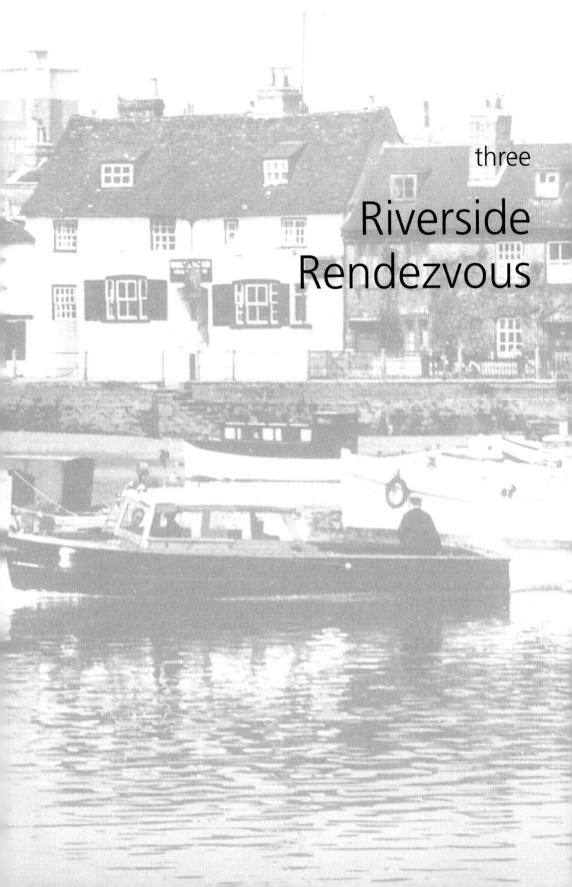

three

Riverside
Rendezvous

Above: The Bell and Crown, Strand on the Green in 1832. Licensed as such by 1787 but probably previously called the Bell, which was licensed by at least 1722. Before the pub served food it would send customers to its near neighbour the City Barge for a meal and the City Barge would send them back for a Scotch (the pub stocked seventeen different varieties in those days).

Below: Frank and Gerardine McBrearty, landlord and landlady of the Bell and Crown, holding the FA Cup in 1992, when Des Lynham was being filmed in the pub.

Right: The then Mayor of Hounslow, Rajinder Singh Bath, with Fuller's dray horses outside the Bell and Crown in 1999. Fuller, Smith & Turner acquired the pub in 1814.

Below: The Bell and Crown in the early 1900s, before it was rebuilt in 1907. In the 1970s it was reputed to have a ghost who made lamps sway, switched off pumps and broke glasses, although he hasn't been seen by the present management. The pub expanded into two adjoining shops in the 1980s and built its large conservatory extension in 1984.

The City Barge, Strand on the Green in 1908. A notice inside the pub claims that it has been in existence since 1484 when it was called the Navigator's Arms. However, it first appears in the licensing lists as the City Navigation Barge in 1787, although previously it was possibly one of two Chiswick pubs called the Bull's Head between 1778 and 1787. In 1940 much of the pub was destroyed by a parachute mine and it was threatened with demolition, but luckily saved. The old bar is all that remains of the original eighteenth-century building. The conservatory extension was added in 1984.

Opposite above: The Brewery Tap, Catherine Wheel Road in 2005. An old beerhouse, it is first mentioned by name in a directory of 1888. Being right beside the canal the pub was the haunt of bargees delivering goods from the London Docks for transhipment by narrowboats along the canal. The present building was put up in 1928 with nine steps up to protect it against possible flooding.

Opposite below: Pub sign of the Brewery Tap, Catherine Wheel Road in 2005. The pub is so-called because it was right beside the Beehive Brewery (*see* Chapter 1). This was acquired by Fuller, Smith & Turner in 1908.

Inn sign of the City Barge. The name of the pub was changed in honour of the City of London Navigation Committee's state barge which was often moored nearby.

Local MP Barney Hayhoe inspecting flood damage at the City Barge in 1978. The footpath outside the pub is frequently flooded.

Drinkers outside the City Barge in 1988. Patrick McHugh, Chris Allsop (?) and Graham Parnum with the crowds that flock to the pub on sunny summer days.

Welcome To One Of Britain's Famous Historic Inns

The City Barge
A. D. 1484

A 500 year Royal Elizabethan Charter Inn on Picturesque Strand on the Green, Chiswick, W. 4., where we offer you hospitality and all that is best of the brewer, vintner and chef in homely warm bars that are dedicated to those splendid fellows who make drinking a pleasure, who reach contentment prior to capacity, and whom, whatever the the drink, can take it, hold it, enjoy it, and remain gentlemen.

LUNCHEONS AND EVENING SNACKS

Mr & Mrs E. Townsend. Tel. Chiswick 2148 & 8649

Advertisement for the City Barge, showing its interior, sometime before 1966. In 2005 the pub belonged to the Spirit Group.

The Bull's Head, Strand on the Green, *c.* 1910. It was licensed by at least 1722 and belonged to Sich's Lamb Brewery, which was taken over by the Isleworth Brewery (*see* Chapter 1), later to Watneys and is now part of the Spirit Group. A notice on the Thames Road frontage of the pub tells us that:

> During the Civil War Oliver Cromwell's sister the Countess of Fauconberg lived nearby and Cromwell was a frequent visitor to the pub. Whilst enjoying the Bull's hospitality Cromwell was betrayed to Royalist troops. However he escaped through a tunnel to an island in the river, which is now known as Oliver's Eyot.

This exciting information has to be taken with a large dollop of scepticism. For a start the Countess of Fauconberg was not Cromwell's sister but his daughter and she didn't move to Chiswick until 1677 (over thirty years after the Civil War).

The Bull's Head in the 1950s. Two of the cottages on the right-hand side were incorporated into the pub in 1972. In the 1960s this pub competed with its neighbour the City Barge in an unusual annual charity event – teams were required to hit golf balls 175 yards across the Thames to land on the Barnes bank.

J. G. WISE,

WATERMAN TO HER MAJESTY,

Wine and Spirit Merchant,

OXFORD AND CAMBRIDGE HOTEL,

KEW BRIDGE, MIDDLESEX.

Dinners and Teas for Private Parties, Clubs, &c.

LARGE & SMALL BOATS FOR PRIVATE PARTIES.

GENTLEMEN'S BOATS TAKEN CARE OF.

Advertisement for the Oxford and Cambridge Hotel, No. 18 Kew Bridge Road in 1877. This small pub was known as the Poplar Inn in 1839 but changed its name in 1867. Popular with the rowing fraternity, it is said to have been the venue for a meeting which made the decision to form a Brentford Football Club in 1889. The Oxford and Cambridge closed in 1923.

Opposite above: The Steam Packet, Strand on the Green in 1972. Café Rouge now occupies the premises of this pub which was licensed by at least 1870. It closed in the early 1980s when it became the Dôme Café.

Opposite below: Paddle steamer close to the Steam Packet (the large building) in the early 1900s. The pub's name comes from the steam launches which used to dock at Kew Pier (put up in 1847) opposite the pub as part of the regular steam packet service up the river.

STRAND-ON-THE-GREEN.   No.414.

THE SHIP INN.   STRAND-ON-GREEN. CHISWICK. 1925.   H.J.WHITMAN.

The Red Lion, Chiswick Mall in the early 1900s. Licensed by at least 1722, the pub stood opposite the Draw Dock where produce such as hops, timber, ships ropes etc. for Chiswick industries was loaded and unloaded (the horse and cart in the water are unloading from the sailing barge). It must have been thirsty work for the carters who transported the goods and for the men who worked the barges. No doubt they regularly patronised the pub. Fuller, Smith & Turner surrendered the licence in 1913 and it became a private residence, now called Red Lion House.

Opposite above: The building that used to be the Ship Inn, Strand on the Green. The pub was licensed by at least 1722 and closed in 1910 when it was converted into a private house, now Ship House.

Opposite below: The yard of the former Ship Inn on a Christmas card of 1925. Some small cottages opened onto the yard in one of which, Ship Cottage, Dylan Thomas used to stay occasionally. The yard still looks much the same although it is now surrounded by a high wall.

The whetstone which used to hang outside the Red Lion. It was used for sharpening tools by the men who cut the osiers (willows used for basket making) on Chiswick Eyot. The whetstone formerly hung outside a pub called the Whetstone and Bear in Chiswick Lane.

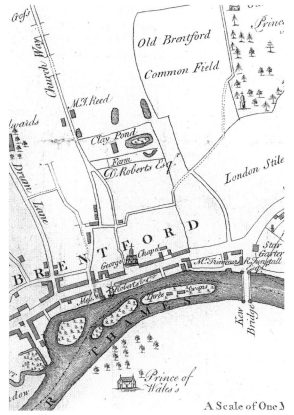

The Three Swans, Brentford Ait. This detail from an Ealing parish map of 1777 shows the position of the pub called the Three Swans or the Swan. Known for its eels and its noisy clientele it was forced to close in the early nineteenth century when an exasperated Kew resident purchased the little island.

Above: The Ferry Hotel/Bunch of Grapes, Ferry Lane, *c.* 1905. This pub beside the old Brentford ferry was built in 1880, replacing a much earlier pub called the Grapes. It might have been in the Grapes that Samuel Pepys in 1665 'ate and drank' before taking a boat from 'Branford to Queenhithe'.

Right: Advertisement for the Ferry Hotel, *c.* 1905. Although the pub seems to have been known as the Ferry Hotel in the 1900s it was always licensed as the Bunch of Grapes. Arthur East was landlord between 1903 and 1909. The licence was surrendered in 1922 and the building used as offices before being razed to the ground between Christmas and New Year 1983 – much to the fury of local residents.

ALIGHT AT THE FIRE STATION, BRENTFORD,

- - for - -

Arthur East's Hotel & Ferry,

For the Waterside Entrance to KEW GARDENS.

"THE FERRY" HOTEL, BRENTFORD.

Boats of every description for Hire by the Hour, Day or Season

AT MODERATE CHARGES.

Private Boats Housed and Repaired.

Luncheons, Dinners and Teas Provided.

The Indian Queen, Strand on the Green before it was demolished in 1907. Licensed by at least 1759, it stood in a large square near Spring Grove and might have been named in honour of Pocahontas who lived for a short time in Brentford. The office building called the Pier House (the Pier House Laundry from 1905-73) is now on its site.

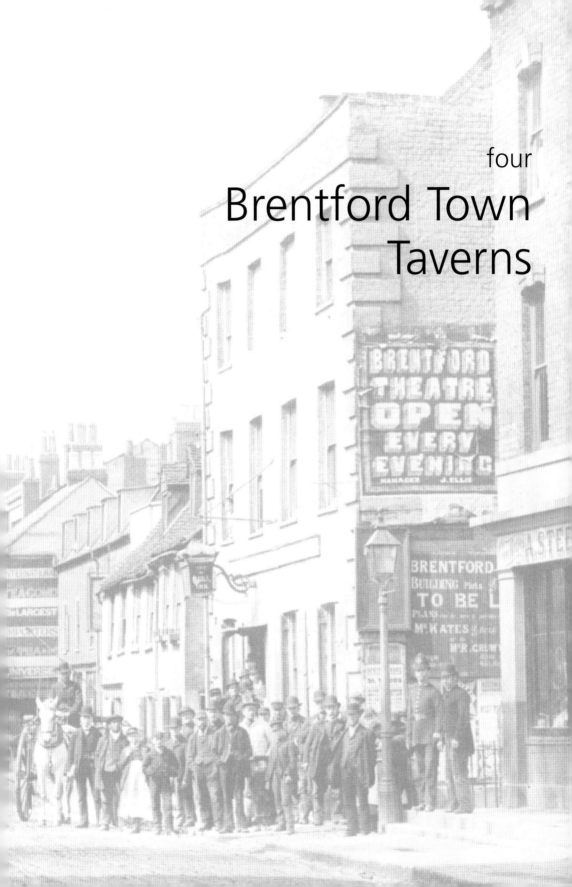

four
Brentford Town
Taverns

Brentford's Fifty

Brentford was so well known for its pubs that a piece of doggerel was written about them. The author starts at the Star and Garter, Kew Bridge Road and proceeds westwards along Brentford High Street, across Brentford Bridge to London Road. Fifty pubs are mentioned. The author is thought to have been one Alfred Pearce, who wrote it in 1948 when he was seventy-four years old (his family ran the Alexandra pub in the High Street). If it is written purely from memory, Mr Pearce did well, but the Brentford trade directories suggest that it is not totally accurate since some of the pubs listed by Mr Pearce had closed before others opened.

> When I was knighted with a STAR AND GARTER
> I was pushed into an EXPRESS
> On my way to OXFORD AND CAMBRIDGE
> I smashed into a PLOUGH
> And stood aside by the WAGGON AND HORSES
> Little beyond a JOLLY TAR
> With a LAMB by his side
> Receiving a SALUTATION
> Presently FOX AND HOUNDS dashed by
> A beautiful HAND AND FLOWER
> When I met the MARQUIS OF GRANBY
> He fell into the QUEEN'S ARMS
> Tugging with a BARGE AGROUND
> A BULL stared me in the face
> As I crossed by the BREWERY TAP and the ROYAL HOTEL
> The PRINCE OF WALES stood the other side
> Up above HALF MOON AND SEVEN STARS
> With a GLITTERING STAR by its side
> Cross yonder stood a DRUM
> Attacked by a LION
> When I reached ALEXANDRA
> I shook hands with GEORGE THE FOURTH
> He advised me to salute THE WATERMAN'S ARMS
> Then I was back in the KING'S ARMS
> Up went the roaring CANNON
> At the RISING SUN I tried to lift ONE TON
> While BRITTANIA stood to one side
> And I met the DUKE OF CAMBRIDGE
> He told me he had lost his FEATHERS
> A little beyond a BEEHIVE
> And a BLACK BOY AND STILL
> Playing with a CATHERINE WHEEL
> As I crossed the BARLEY MOW
> There was a magnificent CASTLE

Near by stood a LION
THREE PIGEONS overhead
With MAGPIE AND STUMP
Beside it MAGPIE AND CROWN
TWO BLACK BOYS were ringing SIX BELLS
Stood staunch THE MAGNET with LORD NELSON
I got into the JUNCTION ARMS
They pushed me into the DUKE OF NORTHUMBERLAND
Beyond stood GEORGE AND DRAGON
The STANDARD floating high
With the ANGEL of peace
When the COACH AND HORSES passed by.

The Albany Arms, Albany Road with the licensee Frederick Coles standing at the entrance, *c.* 1910. It was probably the old beerhouse run by Sarah Nunn in Albany Place in 1853. It was rebuilt by the Royal Brewery (*see* Chapter 1) in 1900 and the inscription 'RBC 1900' can be seen in the stonework above the door.

The Barge Aground, No. 362 Brentford High Street, in 1900. The pub was licensed by 1732 and rebuilt in 1777 when the vestry minutes of St Lawrence's church mention that a pile of bricks for its rebuilding had been left under Mr Roberts's windmill and were required to be removed. The gable behind the pub marks the house where the Methodist preacher John Wesley stayed on his many visits to Brentford.

The Barge Aground in 1961 shortly before it was demolished. The pub stood where the Haverfield Estate is today and was acquired by Fuller, Smith & Turner in 1790. The firm rebuilt it in 1902 but sold part of the premises to the Brentford gasworks in 1924.

The Barley Corn, No. 98 Brentford High Street in 1907. Originally a beerhouse on the corner of Catherine Wheel Yard (now Road) it first appears in a directory of 1853. It closed in 1908.

The Beehive, No. 227 Brentford High Street in 1966. It was licensed by at least 1851 when it was run by William Gomm of the Beehive Brewery (*see* Chapter 1) which initially brewed on a site behind the pub and explains why the pub is so called. It was rebuilt in 1907 to a design by Thomas Henry Nowell Parr and acquired by Fuller, Smith & Turner in 1908. In its early days it catered mainly for travellers and salesmen.

THE "BEEHIVE" HOTEL,

High Street, Brentford.

Proprietor ·   · W. SHOTTER.

THE NEW BUILDING

AT THE

Corner of the Half Acre,

WILL BE

OPENED on **MONDAY NEXT, JULY** 15th.

LUNCHEONS

From 12.30 till 2.30.

DINNERS and TEAS.

Advertisement for the Beehive Hotel in 1907. Announcing the pub's re-opening, the local paper opined that: 'one of the greatest improvements that has ever been made in Brentford is the widening of the Half Acre and the rebuilding of the Bee Hive Hotel'.

The George and Dragon, No. 29 London Road in 2005. This pub first appears in the rate books in 1815 when the landlord was Richard Millard, but may well have been the property belonging to Millard in the rate book for 1790. It was acquired by Fuller, Smith & Turner in 1889, who later sold it to Charrington's.

Lamp outside the George and Dragon.

The Bull, No. 350 Brentford High Street, c. 1886. It stood on the corner of Pottery Road (where the Haverfield Estate is today) and closed around 1961. A pub with this name is recorded as early as 1614. In 1881 it was visited by a writer from the *Licensed Victuallers Gazette* who was astonished by the frescoes adorning the walls. He wrote:

> All round the room are depicted nearly every animal in creation. Over the fireplace is a bodyless trotting horse with a most remarkable sulky behind it, and an equally remarkable looking driver … the tail of this horse seems to have got entangled in the moustachios of the driver and, as far as we could judge, the artist when he painted it must either have been on the verge of delirium tremens or he was handing down to posterity his recollection of a nightmare.

Opposite above: Half-gallon measure from the Bull.

Opposite below: The Brewery Tap, No. 22 Brentford High Street, c. 1905. It first appears in a directory of 1853 when it was known as the Royal Brewery Tap since it was next to, and owned by, the Royal Brewery (*see* Chapter 1). It closed in 1926 to make way for an extension to Brentford's large gasworks (now Watermans Park).

The Half Moon and Seven Stars, No. 25 Brentford High Street from an early nineteenth-century watercolour. It stood where the Watermans Arts Centre is today, was licensed by 1759 and closed around 1903.

The Lord Nelson, Enfield Road in the early 1900s. This old beerhouse has belonged to Fuller, Smith & Turner since 1879 and was reconstructed in 1927. Portraits of Lord Nelson are etched into its windows.

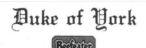

**YORK ROAD
BRENTFORD, MIDDLESEX
Telephone: 01-568 9000**

Postcard advertising the Duke of York, York Road, in the 1980s. The pub was open by at least 1898 and its Victorian ancestry, visible from the rear, is reminiscent of the architecture of Bedford Park. It was renamed the New England in 2001 and its address is now the Great West Road.

The Fox and Hounds, No. 384 Brentford High Street, in 1900. It was licensed by at least 1778 and closed around 1919. Holland Gardens is now on its site.

The Griffin, Brook Road South, *c.* 1942. The pub served as the first clubhouse and changing rooms for Brentford Football Club (formed 1889) and is one of the four pubs on the corners of Griffin Park football ground.

Window glass in the Griffin. The griffin is a heraldic symbol, used in coats of arms, and the trademark of Fuller, Smith & Turner's brewery. The griffins on the pub's roof were melted down for the war effort. A Fuller, Smith & Turner pub since 1883, it was rebuilt in 1903.

Above: Celebrating the opening of a new extension to the Griffin in 2000. Mike Turner and Tim Turner from Fuller, Smith & Turner with local MP Ann Keen and landlady and landlord, Sue Wilson and Ralph Clifton.

Right: The George IV, No. 50 Brentford High Street, after it had ceased to be a pub, *c.* 1950. It was on the eastern corner of Goat Wharf and is first mentioned in a directory of 1848, although it might have had an earlier name. It closed around 1931.

The Drum Inn, No. 319 Brentford High Street, *c.* 1900. It stood on the eastern corner of Ealing Road which was formerly known as Drum Lane. The pub was licensed by at least 1722, altered in 1908 and demolished in 1921 for the widening of Ealing Road. The 1881 census shows that at that date forty people lived at the Drum – the publican James Gomm, his wife, seven children and an assortment of lodgers.

Above: The Princess Royal, Ealing Road, in 2005. One of the four pubs on the corners of Griffin Park football ground, it was built by Fuller, Smith & Turner in 1841. It was rebuilt to a design by Thomas Henry Nowell Parr in 1921. In 2005 Brentford Football Club acquired the tenancy to use the first floor as the club shop.

Right: Lamp outside the Princess Royal.

The Lord Nelson, No. 154 Brentford High Street in the early 1900s, viewed from Brentford Bridge. A pub with that name since at least 1841, it closed in 1904.

The Royal Oak, New Road in the early 1900s. One of the four pubs on the corners of Griffin Park football ground, it first appears in a directory of 1888 and formerly belonged to the Royal Brewery (*see* Chapter 1).

The Feathers, No. 232 Brentford High Street after it closed as a pub in the 1960s. A Brentford pub with this name is first mentioned in 1693 when the Petty Sessions ordered four soldiers to be quartered there. It was acquired by Fuller, Smith & Turner in 1787 and presumably rebuilt. The building was demolished in the early 1980s to make way for what in 2005 is Somerfield's supermarket.

The main bar of the Feathers in 1977 when the pub had become the headquarters of the West London Archaeological Field Group. This photograph shows part of an exhibition of archaeological finds from excavations in Brentford put on by the Group as part of the 1977 Brentford Carnival. Note the window glass, decorated with ostrich feathers (the heraldic badge of the Princes of Wales).

The Express, Kew Bridge Road, *c.* 1903. Originally a beerhouse, the present building was probably put up in the late 1860s. Formerly called the Express Tavern, it was renamed the Express Hotel when R.G. Aldington became the landlord in 1882 and acquired a licence to sell spirits as well as beer and wine. The Aldington family bought the pub in 1922 and have owned it ever since. Beer was supplied by Hawkes & Co. of Bishops Stortford, then by Benskin's which took over Hawkes in 1898. The pub now serves Bass draught and Young's real ales. A market stall set up in the forecourt of the Express in 1888 was the beginning of Brentford's famous wholesale fruit and vegetable market (transferred to Southall in 1974).

Opposite above: The Waggon and Horses, No. 26 Kew Bridge Road in 1921. A pub with this name is recorded in 1759. The Waggon and Horses was acquired by Fuller, Smith & Turner in 1882 and rebuilt in 1937/8.

Opposite below: The Plough, No. 24 Kew Bridge Road in 1992. It stood next door to the rebuilt Waggon and Horses and was demolished in 2000. A Brentford pub called the Plough was licensed by 1722, although it might not have been the pub in the photograph, which was an old beerhouse, recorded in 1853.

The bar of the Express in 1979, the year the pub won the CAMRA award for its Young's real ale. Celebrating are the pub's owners Robert and Hilda Aldington with their son-in-law, Tim Smyth who managed the pub from 1968 to 1994.

The Kew Bowling Club in 'Kozee Korner' outside the Express, *c.* 1905. The pub's large and lovely garden was home to the Bowling Club from 1900 to 1914. Robert G. Aldington, owner of the Express, is in the centre of the front row with his young son Robert S. Aldington on the ground to his right wearing a striped sweater.

Right: Saloon bar of the Express after refurbishment in the 1960s. The pub was just across the road from the Q Theatre which functioned between 1924 and 1956. Actors such as Dirk Bogarde and Kenneth More would often drop in after performances and Charles Hawtrey was sometimes persuaded to play the piano in the bar.

Below: The New Inn, New Road in 2005. This pub on the corner of Boston Manor Road is another of the four pubs on the corners of Griffin Park football ground. It was in existence by at least 1853. The 'New Inn' is actually one of the earliest names given to pubs!

The Globe, Windmill Road in the late twentieth century. It first appears in a directory of 1888 and was acquired by Fuller, Smith & Turner in 1908. Globes are etched into its window glass and there is a globe above the entrance.

The Globe was a winner of the Fuller's Garden Competition in 2003, as well as in earlier years. Here, managers Charlie Fogden and Beata Murray display the winning certificate, presented by Tim Turner of Fuller, Smith & Turner.

The Standard Inn, Half Acre, prior to its demolition in 1897. It is the white building next to the shop selling fish. Probably an old beerhouse, it first appears in a directory of 1853. Brentford's magnificent Vestry Hall was built on its site. This has now been replaced by the less than magnificent police station.

The Seven Stars, Half Acre in the early twentieth century. Licensed by at least 1761 but demolished in 1905 when the Half Acre was widened for the tram route to Hanwell.

The Prince of Wales, No. 346 Brentford High Street, *c.* 1902. The name appears in a directory of 1848 but the building had previously been an older pub called the Running Horses, and before that was known as the Sheepskin Alehouse. In 1881 the walls of the Prince of Wales were adorned with frescoes similar to those at the Bull (*see* page 68). One fresco was signed with the name 'F. Stuart 1872' who was apparently a scene painter for Sangster's Circus. This might explain the many drawings of animals. In 1902 the pub landlord was William Hamblen who, in 1906, became the landlord of the nearby Red Lion. The Prince of Wales was a Fuller's pub and closed in 1908. The building was demolished and the Haverfield Estate is now on its site.

Opposite above: The King's Arms, Boston Manor Road in 1904. Possibly the pub licensed as the Little King's Arms by 1792 (to distinguish it from the Great King's Arms at No. 273 Brentford High Street) but certainly on its present site by 1840. It formerly belonged to the Isleworth Brewery which purchased Chiswick's Lamb Brewery (*see* Chapter 1). The pub was altered and extended in the 1930s.

Opposite below: The Magpie and Crown, No. 128 Brentford High Street in 1969. This might have been the pub called the Pye, recorded in 1614, where four horses and men of His Majesty's Regiment of Horse Guards were stationed in 1709. Recorded as the Magpie and Crown by 1722, it once belonged to Chiswick's Lamb Brewery (*see* Chapter 1). It has been rebuilt and is now a free house.

Above: The Red Lion, No. 318 Brentford High Street in 1965. It was on the western corner of Ealing Road and in existence since at least 1669, when the magistrates ordered the landlord, Thomas Warburton, to 'pull down the post of his sign standing on the highway or be committed until he does.' The pub was acquired by Fuller, Smith & Turner in 1836, rebuilt in 1907 and closed in 1965.

Left: Tankard with the inscription 'RED LION OLD BRENTFORD' on the base. The initials on the side are those of William Hamblen, the pub's landlord between 1906 and 1933.

Right: The Red Lion, No. 322 Brentford High Street in 1972. This pub was built in 1965 on the eastern corner of Ealing Road to replace the pub pictured on page 86. It won the *Evening Standard* Pub of the Year Award in 1967 and was well known for its live music. McDonald's purchased the site in 1996, demolished the pub and replaced it with the present eaterie.

Below: The Marquis of Granby, No. 369 Brentford High Street in the early 1900s. This small pub was sandwiched between the stone-built St George's church and the shop advertising Zebra polish which belonged at the time to George Knight, oil and colourman. The pub first appears in a licensing list of 1772 and closed in 1903 to make way for an extension to the Brentford gasworks (Holland Gardens is now on its site).

The Six Bells, No. 149 Brentford High Street in the 1890s. Licensed by at least 1722, and leased by Fuller, Smith & Turner from 1815 (purchased in 1873), it was rebuilt in 1904. In 1835 a coroner's inquest was held in the Six Bells on one John Moody, driver of a stagecoach who, together with his passengers, was 'precipitated' over Brentford Bridge and into the water.

Darts contest at the Six Bells, 2001. Eric Bristow with the darts team, from left to right: Richie Gardener, Charlie Holdaway, Tim Steadman and Robbie Day, winners of the London Pride Heineken Darts Classic Championship.

The North Star, North Road in 1966. Licensed by at least 1853 and demolished in 2002. It was known in the 1970s for the darts prowess of its punters.

The North Star in the 1990s, by which time it had become a club.

The Salutation Inn, No. 401 Brentford High Street, at the end of the nineteenth century. It was licensed by at least 1727 and closed in 1919. A petrol station now occupies its site.

Opposite above: The Hand and Flower, No. 379 Brentford High Street, in the early 1900s. Licensed by at least 1765, it closed around 1904 and Holland Gardens now covers its site.

Opposite below: The Pottery Arms, Clayponds Lane in 1971. Its name comes from the fact that it stood near a large pottery. It first appears in a directory of 1888, was rebuilt in 1921/2 to a design by Thomas Henry Nowell Parr, and purchased by Fuller, Smith & Turner in 1928. This photograph was taken the year the pub was threatened with demolition. Fortunately it was saved.

Left: The Waterman's Arms, Ferry Lane in 2005. The pub has been in existence since at least 1751 and was rebuilt in the twentieth century. It formerly belonged to Watney's.

Below: The One Tun, No. 254 Brentford High Street in 1905. This forlorn-looking pub with stabling behind was demolished shortly after this photograph was taken. It had been in existence since at least 1787. It was previously called the Two (or Jolly) Sawyers and, before that, the Chopping Knife and Tun, recorded in 1751. Between 1839 and 1901 it was run by one family called Thick. Its site is now covered by Somerfield's car park.

Above: The Windmill, Orchard Road. Licensed by at least 1853 it closed in 1999 when the building was demolished for a development of flats (not yet erected in 2005).

Right: The Royal Horseguardsman, Ealing Road in 2005. An old beerhouse, it first appears in a directory of 1888 as the Horseguardsman. Its tiled entrance step bears the legend 'Ashby's Ales' which was a Staines brewery.

The White Horse, Market Place in 1911. This pub is mentioned in the Church Burial Register of 1603 which records the demise of one George Wood 'dwelinge at the sign of the White Horse in the market place'. The house on the left in the picture is on the site of the home of Joseph Mallord William Marshall, the uncle of the artist J.M.W. Turner. Turner lived here with his uncle for about a year when he was ten years old.

Opposite above: Interior of the White Horse in 1959 with Mrs Adams the landlady and a customer. The pub was acquired by Fuller, Smith & Turner in 1863 who sold it to Charrington's. It is now (2005) privately owned and has been called the Weir since 2004.

Opposite below: The Magnet, No. 152 Brentford High Street in the early 1900s. This pub on the corner of the Ham was in existence by at least 1881. It ceased to be a pub in 1955 and the building was used as offices, latterly by Ballancroft Film and TV Equipment, before being demolished in the 1980s.

Left: The Northumberland Arms, No. 11 London Road in the 1990s. A pub since at least 1853 and now a free house. It was put up for sale in 2005.

Below: Stripes Bar in 2004. This has been the bar of the Brentford Football Club since 1965. The performers on stage are author Robert Rankin and his band the Rock Gods. The figure with the baseball cap is Brentford local councillor Luke Kirton.

Above: The Bricklayers' Arms, Ealing Road in 1965. This pub has been immortalised as the 'Flying Swan' in Robert Rankin's fantasy stories set in Brentford. A Brentford pub called the Bricklayers' Arms is recorded in 1853. In the 1960s and '70s it was a jazz pub, after a then little-known group called the Temperance Seven used it for practice sessions.

Right: The Royal Hotel, No. 27 Brentford High Street in 1900. It was built around 1828 by Sir Felix Booth, proprietor of the Royal Brewery (*see* Chapter 1). The hotel was demolished in 1927 to make way for an extension to Brentford's large gasworks. Watermans Arts Centre now occupies the site.

The Rising Sun, Nos 68–69 Brentford High Street in the 1960s. Licensed by at least 1763, it was acquired by Fuller, Smith & Turner in 1908. It closed in 1959 and the building is now (2005) part of Fat Boys Restaurant.

O'Riordan's, No. 3 Brentford High Street, in the 1990s. Now (2005) called Captain Morgan's it first appears in a directory of 1888 as the Royal Tar.

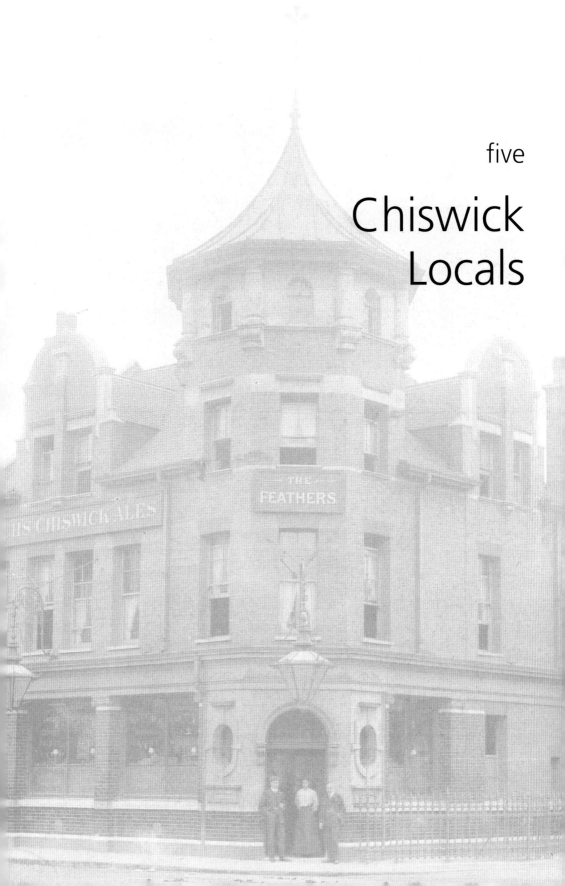

five

Chiswick
Locals

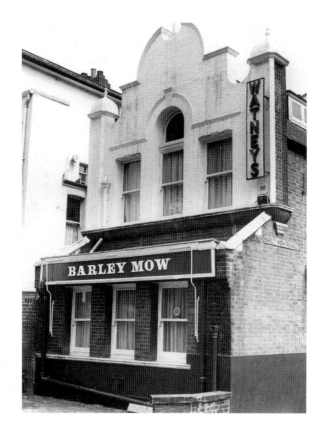

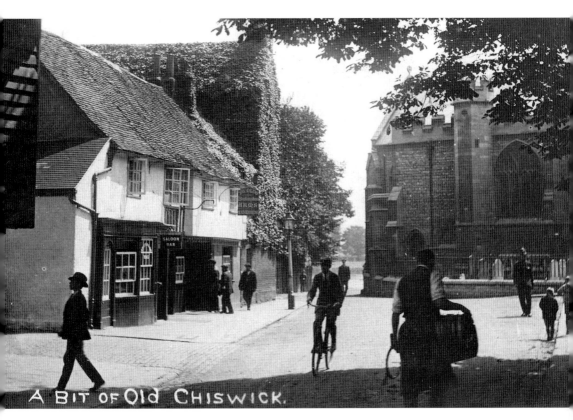

A BIT OF Old CHISWICK.

The Burlington Arms, Church Street in the 1920s. Now converted into two houses this is probably the oldest building in Chiswick, apart from the tower of St Nicholas church. The structure dates from at least the sixteenth century (an Elizabethan sixpence was found under the floorboards) and it had become a pub by at least 1732. The building is reputed to be haunted by a tall man with a large wide-brimmed hat who disarranges the pictures and is nicknamed Percy. The pub's licence was surrendered in 1924 and transferred to the Western Avenue Hotel, Acton.

Opposite above: The Barley Mow, Barley Mow Passage, in 1972. Licensed by at least 1761 a painted sign on the side wall (now practically illegible) shows that the pub once belonged to Chiswick's Lamb Brewery (*see* Chapter 1). Actor Jack Warner (TV cop Dixon of Dock Green) was a one time regular in this pub which now belongs to the Spirit Group.

Opposite below: The Barley Mow from Chiswick High Road in 2005. An 1976 article described the pub as 'off the beaten track' but this was no longer the case once the entrance from the High Road through a garden was constructed in 1983. The white building behind the pub is the wallpaper factory C.F.A. Voysey designed for Sanderson in 1902/3.

Above: The Burlington Arms with the Lamb Brewery (*see* Chapter 1) behind. The pub belonged to this brewery.

Left: Detail of the building now known as the Old Burlington, once the pub called the Burlington Arms.

Right: Doorway of the Old Burlington (the former Burlington Arms). Outside the pub is a cupboard which is said to have been where drunks were locked in until they sobered up.

Below: The Bolton Hotel, No. 81 Duke Road, in the early 1900s. This pub was built sometime before 1882 to serve the Glebe Estate and was called the Bolton Hotel and Music Hall in *Kelly's Directory* of 1893. The pub closed in 1995 and the building is now residential.

The Coach and Horses, No. 29 Chiswick High Road before 1900. Described as 'a humble old roadside inn' it was licensed by at least 1759 and was popular with the drivers of market carts and hay wagons travelling to London. The 'humble' inn was demolished in 1900 and replaced by a 'palatial' building which, in 2005, was the restaurant called Est, Est, Est.

The Coach and Horses in 1972 when it had become a Schooner Inn, complete with stream. 'The only pub in London where you have to walk over a stream to get to the main bar', said a newspaper article in 1976. The boards on the front of the pub were painted gaudy shades of pink and pale green and had to be removed after complaints from residents.

Inn sign for the Coach and Horses, 1983. No conventional hanging sign for this pub but a full-size model of a coach on its first floor balcony. In 1992 the pub was converted into Jo Smo's Bar and Diner, and changed to Nacho's Mexican restaurant in 1994.

The Duke of York, Devonshire Road in 2005. It was in existence by at least 1834 when it was acquired by Fuller, Smith & Turner which rebuilt it to a design by Thomas Henry Nowell Parr in 1927.

The Crown and Anchor, No. 374 Chiswick High Road in 1863. The pub appears to have been built sometime before 1839. In 1992 manager, Andy Bennett, escaped serious injury when he opened a packet which exploded in his hands. It had been sent by the Mardi Gras bomber, Edward Pearce, who made bombs in his Chiswick garden shed in an attempt to extort money from large firms.

The Crown and Anchor in the early 1900s. The pub had been altered and given a ground-floor extension in 1882 (and has been reconstructed since). It was the only pub in Chiswick belonging to Wandsworth brewer, Young and Co., but in 2005 Young's sold it to the Capital Pub Co.

The Crown and Anchor in 2001, a watercolour by Catherine Masterman.

"Gardener's Arms,"

Gunnersbury. ❀

ROYAL BREWERY
FINE ALES AND STOUT.

Electric Cars within few yards.

Accommodation for Parties.

Advertisement for the Gardener's Arms, No. 515 Chiswick High Road, *c.* 1905. It stood on what is now the south-west corner of Chiswick Roundabout and first appears in a directory of 1888. It was demolished in 1957 to make way for an enlargement of the roundabout.

Above: The Duke of Sussex on the corner of Beaconsfield Road and Acton Lane in the late nineteenth century. Now called the Duke, it was a beerhouse by at least 1842. In 1902 the publican was charged with diluting the beer.

Below: The Duke of Sussex, *c.* 1905. The earlier pub had been rebuilt in 1898 and now belonged to the Cannon Brewery Co. of Clerkenwell. This small brewery acquired 125 pubs between 1893 and 1898, most of which it rebuilt. This pub still retains some of its original cut glass. In 1989 it was a Taylor Walker house and is now (2005) a Firkin's pub.

Right: The Pilot, Wellesley Road in 1972. The pub was built sometime before 1869 as a local for the residents of the large houses put up in the area by Adam Askew during the 1860s. It won the Best Kept Pub award in 1976, became a gastro-pub, and was acquired by Fuller, Smith & Turner in 2005.

Below: The Emperor, No. 232 Chiswick High Road, in 1911. It is the tall building to the left of the sign for A.J. Fowkes and first appears in a directory of 1888. Around 1961 Marks & Spencer acquired the premises for an extension and the pub moved to Nos 304–306. Regulars remember it as having a convenient back door (very useful for after hours drinking!). The pub closed in the 1990s.

The Feathers, Hogarth Lane, in the early 1900s. Licensed by at least 1722 and belonging to the Lamb Brewery (*see* Chapter 1) it was rebuilt in the Victorian era but demolished to make way for the A4 and Hogarth Roundabout in the late 1950s. It was replaced with a pub of the same name on the north side of the roundabout in 1960 but this has now been demolished and the TVR car showroom built on its site.

The Grove Park Hotel, Grove Park Road in 1910. It was built in 1867 as the first building on the new Grove Park estate of houses for the professional middle class. It now (2005) belongs to the Spirit Group.

GROVE PARK HOTEL

(NEAR CHISWICK RAILWAY STATION).

Proprietor ··· **WILLIAM PARMENTER.**

BASS'S ALES & GUINNESS'S STOUT.

SUPERIOR BRANDIES, WHISKIES, & OTHER SPIRITS.

Lemonade, Soda and Seltzer Waters.

GOOD BILLIARD TABLE.

BED ROOMS AND SITTING ROOMS.

An advertisement for the Grove Park Hotel in 1877. The hotel was right by Chiswick railway station (opened 1849) and was designed to attract visitors who wished to take part in Chiswick's riverside activities.

Above: The White Swan, Bennett Street in 1977 with landlord and landlady, John and Ida Sweetman. An old beerhouse, it was probably on this site since at least 1847. In the 1920s it was famous for its linnet-singing competitions. When the black cloth on top of the caged birds was removed the linnets began to sing and customers placed bets on which bird would sing the longest.

Below: The building that used to be the White Swan, Bennett Street, in 2005. It can be seen from the A4 opposite the gate to Hogarth's House. Charringtons sold the pub in the early 1980s and it was converted into offices in 1983.

Above: The Railway Hotel, Bollo Lane in the early 1900s. The barrels on the pavement suggest that a beer delivery is being made. A pub since 1880, its name was changed to the Railway Tavern then, around 1988, to the Orange Kipper. By 2001 it was called the Bollo House and in 2005 is just the Bollo.

Right: Painting of a locomotive on the wall of the Railway Tavern in 1975. This replaced the Huggins sign in the picture above but has now been painted over.

The Lamb Tap, Church Street, in the early 1900s. Now Lamb Cottage, a private house, it was a pub – initially called the Lamb – from at least 1732 to 1909. It was in the Lamb Tap that an inquest was held in 1889 on Montague Druitt who had drowned in the Thames. Druitt is one of many suspects for the Jack the Ripper murders.

Opposite above: The Lamb Tap after its closure in 1909 and the Burlington Arms (closed 1924). Both pubs belonged to Sich's Lamb Brewery which was at their rear.

Opposite below: The Manor Tavern in Devonshire Road in 2005 when it had become the Devonshire House gastro-pub. It first appears in a directory of 1888 and was behind a grand seventeenth-century mansion known as Manor Farm House, hence the pub's name. In the early twentieth century this pub was famous for its boxing matches. The present building, designed by Thomas Henry Nowell Parr, was put up in 1924.

The George and Devonshire, Burlington Lane, *c.* 1912. The present eighteenth-century listed building replaced an earlier pub known as the George which in 1791 was acquired by John Thompson of what was to later become the Griffin Brewery (*see* Chapter 1). In 1775 the Mayor of London invited over 300 Middlesex freeholders to a feast in the George. By 1826 'Devonshire' had been added to the pub name and the arms of the Dukes of Devonshire are displayed on its hanging sign. All the buildings on the left in this picture, up to the Post and Telegraph Office, were demolished when the present A316 was constructed in the 1930s.

Opposite above: The Prince of Wales, No. 179 Chiswick High Road, in the 1920s. It was licensed by at least 1792 and rebuilt in the 1930s. It closed as a pub in 1961 when it was converted into flats with business premises below (occupied in 2005 by bookmakers Ladbrokes).

Opposite below: Plumes of ostrich feathers (the emblem of the Princes of Wales) on the front of the building that used to be the Prince of Wales pub.

The John Bull, No. 590 Chiswick High Road, in the early 1900s. The pub was built in 1853 with a saloon next door (put up a few years later) with tables for billiards, pool and 'pyramids' (snooker). It was converted into a Truman Gateway pub in 1972. In 2004 the pub was sold to the Spirit Group and in 2005 was about to be incorporated into a new housing development.

TELEPHONE 62 CHISWICK.

John Bull Hotel,

LIVERY & BAIT STABLES.

Landau, Victorias and Brougham.
Cabs at Shortest Notice. ∴ ∴

AT LOWEST POSSIBLE PRICES.

High Road, Gunnersbury.

OPPOSITE STATION.

An advertisement for the John Bull in 1913/14. For many years the pub has been known for its live music where groups such as The Who performed.

The Hole in the Wall, Sutton Lane as it was thought to have looked in 1780. Licensed by at least 1722 as the Queen's Head, it was rebuilt in 1925. In the nineteenth century it acquired the nickname 'the hole in the wall' reputedly because the landlord knocked a hole in one of the walls to gain easier access to the animals he kept across the road. However, Hole in the Wall is quite a common pub name.

The Studio Club, Woodstock Road, *c.* 1989. Owner David Virgo (centre) and regular customers Helen Slater and Simon Quinn are propping up the bar in this tiny private club. Formed in 1953 as a bridge club it was a popular drinking venue in the days when the pubs closed at 3.30 p.m.

Above: The Fox and Hounds/ Mawson Arms, Chiswick Lane South, in 1957 when the Hogarth Roundabout was being constructed. This pub has two names because Fuller, Smith & Turner amalgamated two separate licences on the brewery site in 1899 when the premises were extended.

Left: Plaque on the Mawson Arms to the poet, essayist and writer, Alexander Pope, who lived in this house, a listed building, with his parents between 1716 and 1719.

Right: Inn sign of the Fox and Hounds which was licensed by at least 1759 as the Fox and Dogs. It was acquired by Fuller, Smith & Turner in 1860 when it was located further down Chiswick Lane. It moved to its present site in 1898 and in 1899 the licence was transferred to the Fox and Hounds and Mawson Arms.

Below: The Fox and Hounds/Mawson Arms in 2005. The building that contains the Mawson Arms became a pub in 1899.

The Windmill, No. 214 Chiswick High Road, in the 1880s. Licensed as the Windmill and Wheatsheaf by at least 1722, the Windmill and Swan by 1765 but just the Windmill in a directory of 1839, it was acquired by Fuller, Smith & Turner in 1802. On the front of the pub is a sundial bearing the date 1717 with the motto 'So flies life away'. When the building was demolished the sundial was found to have been made of plaster, not stone as originally thought, so it did not survive the rebuilding.

Opposite above: The Windmill in the early 1900s. The building in the previous picture was demolished around 1900 and replaced with this grandiose Victorian edifice. The pub was so named because it stood near the windmill north of the High Road shown on a road map of 1675.

Opposite below: The Windmill in 1975. The Victorian pub was pulled down in 1964 to make way for an office block with the pub incorporated below. The office building was, for many years, the headquarters of fast-food chain Wimpy but is now flats. The Windmill was renamed Jack Stamp's Beerhouse in the mid-1990s but closed in 2005 when it became Balan's restaurant.

Above: The Tabard, Bath Road, *c.* 1906. Designed by R. Norman Shaw and built in 1880 this pub was one of the public buildings put up to serve the new Bedford Park estate, which was intended to be a self-contained community. The Tabard served as Bedford Park's pub, restaurant and hotel.

Below: Norman Shaw's original design for the Tabard (here called 'ye hostelry') which appeared in *Building News* in January 1880. The Tabard, a Grade II★ listed building, is important in the history of pub architecture since it was one of the first of a new breed of pubs intended to invoke the village inns of earlier years and as a reaction against Victorian architecture of the time.

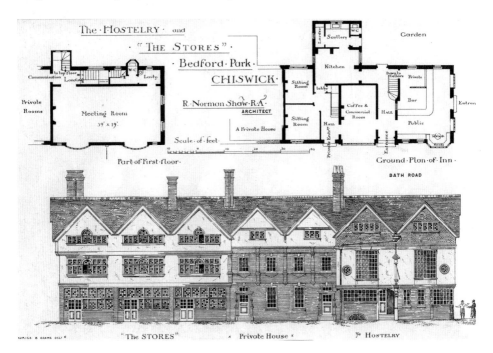

Above: Tiles by William de Morgan in the Tabard, photographed in 2005. The design of Bedford Park was influenced by the Aesthetic Movement of the 1870s and aesthetic artists such as William de Morgan and Walter Crane were employed to enhance the pub's interior decoration.

Right: Fireplace in the Tabard, with tiles by the artist Walter Crane, in 2005.

Watercolour of the Tabard by T.M. Rooke, 1883. The pre-Raphaelite artist, Rooke, lived in Bedford Park and painted the pub's original inn sign. The picture shown here used to hang inside the pub but unfortunately it was stolen in the 1980s. The author of this book would welcome any information as to its present whereabouts.

Above: The Robin Hood and Little John can be espied behind the billboards. This pub, opened by 1862, displayed above its door the slogan: 'Try Charrington's ale, you will find it good/ Step in and drink with Robin Hood/If Robin Hood be not at home/Come in and drink with Little John'. These buildings were demolished in 1896.

Right: The building at No. 450 Chiswick High Road that was put up in 1897 for the Robin Hood and Little John pub (the words 'Robin Hood' can just be seen in the top stonework). The pub became Tommy Flynn's Bar around 2003.

Index of Illustrations